Discount Justice

State Court Belt-Tightening in an Era of Fiscal Austerity

Michael D. Greenberg, Samantha Cherney

For more information on this publication, visit www.rand.org/t/CF343

Library of Congress Cataloging-in-Publication Data is available for this publication.
ISBN: 978-0-8330-9783-5

Published by the RAND Corporation, Santa Monica, Calif.

© Copyright 2017 RAND Corporation

RAND® is a registered trademark.

Cover image: Wikimedia Commons/Photochick234

Preface

In the years following the 2008 financial crisis, media accounts of state courthouse closures, judicial vacancies, and reductions in court services have become widespread. Continuing fiscal pressure on the states has led to corresponding pressure for court system retrenchment. Less clear is whether the adaptation of the courts to the new fiscal environment has led to more sustainable funding and operating models for state court systems. A series of related policy questions follows: How confident are we that state courts can continue to operate during periods of severe economic disruption? Did the adjustment of the courts to post-2008 fiscal conditions result in any basic change to access to justice or to the nature and quality of the services provided by the courts? And for the future, how can we ensure that state courts will retain their fundamental identity and purpose and continue to be available when we need them most?

On January 12, 2015, the UCLA–RAND Center for Law and Public Policy held a conference in Santa Monica, California, to address these questions. Panelists at the event sought to examine the depth of the resourcing problem for state courts, discuss impact and collateral implications, and identify policy options and practical steps that could be taken to mitigate the challenges. Invited participants included judges, state court administrators, prominent members of the bar, and legal scholars.

This report shares key issues and topics from the January 2015 conference sessions. This document is not a transcript. Rather, it summarizes the panel discussions and major points made by the participants, as well as their responses during question-and-answer sessions with the conference audience. These proceedings should be of broad interest to the judicial and legal communities, policymakers with an interest in the justice system, and participants in the justice system more broadly.

About the UCLA–RAND Center for Law and Public Policy

The mission of the UCLA–RAND Center for Law and Public Policy is to inform legal and public policymakers with innovative legal scholarship grounded in multidisciplinary empirical analysis. The center fosters collaborative research, holds conferences, and trains law students in the Empirical Legal Scholars program. It is the first center of its kind to create a partnership between a law school and a major nonprofit research institute.

Founded in 1949, the University of California, Los Angeles, School of Law is the youngest top-ranked law school in the nation and has established a tradition of innovation in its approach to teaching, research, and scholarship.

The RAND Institute for Civil Justice (ICJ) is dedicated to improving the civil justice system by supplying policymakers and the public with rigorous and nonpartisan research. Its studies identify trends in litigation and inform policy choices about liability, compensation, regulation, risk management, and insurance. ICJ builds on a long tradition of RAND Corporation research characterized by an interdisciplinary, empirical approach to public policy issues and rigorous standards of quality, objectivity, and independence. All its publications are subject to peer review and disseminated widely to policymakers, practitioners in law and business, other researchers, and the public.

ICJ is part of RAND Justice, Infrastructure, and Environment, a division of the RAND Corporation. This division is dedicated to improving policy and decisionmaking in a wide range of policy domains, including civil and criminal justice, infrastructure protection and homeland security, transportation and energy policy, and environmental and natural resource policy. For more information about the UCLA–RAND Center for Law and Public Policy or the RAND Institute for Civil Justice, visit www.rand.org/icj or contact the director at icjdirector@rand.org.

RAND Ventures

RAND is a research organization that develops solutions to public policy challenges to help make communities throughout the world safer and more secure, healthier and more prosperous. RAND is nonprofit, nonpartisan, and committed to the public interest.

RAND Ventures is a vehicle for investing in policy solutions. Philanthropic contributions support our ability to take the long view, tackle tough and often-controversial topics, and share our findings in innovative and compelling ways. RAND's research findings and recommendations are based on data and evidence, and therefore do not necessarily reflect the policy preferences or interests of its clients, donors, or supporters.

This venture was funded by generous contributions of the RAND Institute for Civil Justice Board of Overseers and other donors to ICJ, as well as by the following event sponsors: Brad Brian and Munger, Tolles & Olson LLP; Dickstein Shapiro LLP; the Foundation of the International Association of Defense Counsel; Jeff Kichaven Commercial Litigation; and Robins Kaplan LLP.

Contents

Summary

In the years following the 2008 financial crisis, media accounts of state courthouse closures, judicial vacancies, and reductions in court services have become widespread. Continuing fiscal pressure on the states has led to corresponding pressure for court system retrenchment. Less clear is whether the adaptation of the courts to the new fiscal environment has led to more sustainable funding and operating models for state court systems. A series of related policy questions follows: How confident are we that state courts can continue to operate during periods of severe economic disruption? Did the adjustment of the courts to post-2008 fiscal conditions result in any basic change to access to justice or to the nature and quality of services provided by the courts? And for the future, how can we ensure that state courts will retain their fundamental identity and purpose and continue to be available when we need them most?

On January 12, 2015, the UCLA–RAND Center for Law and Public Policy held a conference in Santa Monica, California, to address these questions. A series of panel discussions and keynote speeches at the event sought to examine the depth of the resourcing problem for state courts, discuss impact and collateral implications, and identify policy options and practical steps that could be taken to mitigate the challenges. The conference also sought to examine the availability of empirical evidence pertaining to state court resourcing challenges and to identify questions and opportunities for future research. Invited participants included judges, state court administrators, prominent members of the bar, and legal scholars.

Keynote speeches at the conference were given by Tani G. Cantil-Sakauye, the Chief Justice of California, and by William T. Robinson III, co-chair of the American Bar Association (ABA) Task Force on Preservation of the Justice System and former president of the ABA. Their remarks appear in Chapters Four and Seven, respectively, of this report.

The initial panel discussion focused on financing, governance, and the current state of state courts. Major topics of conversation included the variation in state court funding mechanisms and changes following the 2008 financial crisis, the governance structure of the court system in Minnesota and how it compares to that of other states, how court systems seek to modify operations when responding to budget cuts, and the likely long-term effects for state court systems associated with the budget cuts they experienced post-2008.

The second panel discussion examined the constitutional dimensions of the funding of state courts. Major focal points in that session included when and how constitutional principles are implicated in the funding of state courts, whether the relevant landscape for constitutional challenge has changed in recent years, whether there is a conflict of interest and potential for delegitimization of the courts in connection with judges deciding these sorts of constitutional disputes, and whether empirical data have a role to play in discussions of constitutional adequacy of court system funding.

The third panel discussion focused on empirical research findings pertinent to the resourcing of state courts. The panelists described their own research findings pertaining to court resourcing and reviewed empirical studies and methodological issues that shed light on court resourcing issues. The panelists then responded to questions from the audience concerning their remarks.

The topic of the final panel discussion was access to justice and business-to-business litigation. Craig Holden spoke broadly to the impact of the court resourcing crisis in California on the state's business community. Rebecca Sandefur described the results of survey research on civil court utilization by the public and, by inference, the impact of post-2008 austerity budgets on access to justice. Jeff Kichaven spoke about alternatives to court-based adjudication for civil disputes and his views that court-affiliated alternative dispute resolution mediation programs should be discontinued in California in favor of private mediation services. The panelists also responded to questions from the audience following their remarks.

Acknowledgments

The UCLA–RAND Center for Law and Public Policy would like to thank the panelists, speakers, and all those who engaged in the conference discussions. We would particularly like to thank the following participants for their contribution to the panels and the discussion, without which the conference would not have been feasible: Joseph Doherty, Judge Carolyn Kuhl, Mary McQueen, Minnesota Chief Justice Lorie Skjerven Gildea, Robert Peck, New York Chief Judge Jonathan Lippman, Donna Melby, M.C. Sungaila, Thomas M. Clarke, Ingrid Eagly, Herbert Kritzer, Geoff McGovern, Paul Heaton, Rebecca Sandefur, Craig Holden, and Jeff Kichaven. In addition, we would like to thank California Chief Justice Tani G. Cantil-Sakauye and William T. Robinson III for their keynote addresses to the conference attendees.

Finally, we extend special thanks to the donors and supporters who made this conference and the work of the RAND Institute for Civil Justice (ICJ) possible. Sponsors who generously provided philanthropic support of the conference and these proceedings are Brad Brian and Munger, Tolles & Olson LLP; Dickstein Shapiro LLP; the Foundation of the International Association of Defense Counsel; Jeff Kichaven Commercial Litigation; and Robins Kaplan LLP. Special thanks are due to ICJ Overseers Robert Peck and M.C. Sungaila for their tireless efforts in bringing this conference to fruition and for making it a productive dialogue.

CHAPTER ONE

Introduction and Introductory Remarks

In the years following the 2008 financial crisis, media accounts of state courthouse closures, judicial vacancies, and reductions in court services have become widespread. Continuing fiscal pressure on the states has led to corresponding pressure for court system retrenchment. Less clear is whether the adaptation of the courts to the new fiscal environment has led to more-sustainable funding and operating models for state court systems. A series of related policy questions follows: How confident are we that state courts can continue to operate during periods of severe economic disruption? Did the adjustment of the courts to post-2008 fiscal conditions result in any basic change to access to justice or to the nature and quality of services provided by the courts? And for the future, how can we ensure that state courts will retain their fundamental identity and purpose and continue to be available when we need them most?

On January 12, 2015, the UCLA–RAND Center for Law and Public Policy held a conference in Santa Monica, California, to address these questions. A series of panel discussions and keynote speeches at the event sought to examine the depth of the resourcing problem for state courts, discuss impact and collateral implications, and identify policy options and practical steps that could be taken to mitigate the challenges. Invited participants included judges, state court administrators, prominent members of the bar, and legal scholars.

The current report is organized by chapters, which correspond to the panel discussions and speeches that took place during the conference. Each of the panel discussions is summarized by the major themes that were discussed in the order that they were covered at the conference event. The introductory and keynote speeches presented at the conference are also included in this report.

Opening of the Conference

The conference event was opened by Paul Heaton, then director of the RAND Institute for Civil Justice, and Laura Gómez, vice dean of the UCLA School of Law, with subsequent introductory remarks by Michael Greenberg. Heaton and Gómez introduced the two hosting institutions, respectively, and described their shared interest in empirical research and multidisciplinary scholarship on the U.S. civil justice system. Heaton then framed the rationale for this conference event, spotlighting the importance of an effective judiciary for a democratic society and the potential for the deleterious impact of resourcing problems on court system effectiveness. Heaton observed that empirical questions about the basic value proposition of the courts were timely, in the wake of post-2008 resourcing cuts to the courts. As the U.S. economy bounced back from recession several years later, courts began to advocate to recover the funding that had been lost during the downturn. Heaton suggested that the successfulness of that advocacy would depend on data and analysis documenting the value return of various forms of investment in courts and any functional decrement that had occurred as a result of reductions in funding.

Following his opening remarks, Heaton briefly reviewed the conference agenda and explained the format of the day's moderated panel discussions. Heaton then introduced Michael Greenberg from RAND as the conference's lead-off speaker. A transcript of Greenberg's remarks follows.

Introductory Remarks by Michael Greenberg

Good morning. My name is Michael Greenberg, and I am a longtime research analyst with RAND and the Institute for Civil Justice. I am also one of the people at RAND who is particularly interested in the issue of judicial branch resourcing. Along with Geoffrey McGovern of RAND and Joseph Doherty at UCLA, we have been in an extended conversation for several years on this topic, and talking about future research projects that we might do on this. It's very gratifying to have you all here today, to share some of our own thinking and work on judicial branch financing and governance issues, and also to learn from all of you in talking about these issues.

I thought I'd start by putting a human face on what we're going to be talking about today. A couple of weeks ago I was at a cocktail party with some friends, none of whom are lawyers, judges, or connected to RAND. And somebody asked me, "What are you working on now, and what excites you about it?" And I replied, "There are two things that have been on my mind lately. One of them is the institutional administration and governance of state court systems. The other is accounting." And the three people I was talking to nearly collapsed [with boredom].

And it struck me that that reaction is a fundamental part of the problem that we're now facing as a society. The fact is that court system financing and governance are important issues of public policy. They're issues that potentially impact all of us in our daily lives. This is something that is salient to those of us who have spent time thinking about this, and especially to those of us who practice in law or in the judiciary, but it's not so salient to the public as a whole. So one of the things we need to do is to make the case, and to make it intuitive and accessible, about why these issues matter more broadly.

So in five minutes, I am going to take a shot at making the case. Why are those two things, institutional governance and administration of the courts and accounting, important?

So let's start with the institutional governance of court systems. Am I safe in assuming that everybody in this room went to law school? Are we all lawyers here? No. I see heads shaking. Show of hands: How many of you went to law school? Okay, everybody except the two of you. *[Laughter from the audience.]*

So how many of you, when you were going to law school, felt that constitutional law was one of your favorite classes? Fair number, right? So, constitutional law is sort of emblematic of the intellectual and philosophical foundations of law more generally. It's the collision of political philosophy with trying to write down on paper meaningful codes, meaningful words, that are going to govern how we live. Words that will deal with the big-picture issues of how authority is divided, and what kind of rights we have as individuals, and how we separate powers and ensure checks and balances, and how we protect procedural due process, and all of that kind of stuff.

Among other things, the Constitution establishes that the judiciary is supposed to perform certain functions and to be organized in a certain way. And many of our other laws follow in that same kind of spirit. They have meaning. They set out principles that are supposed to influence the way that society functions and that are supposed to protect us.

In the years since leaving law school, I have had the experience that there's something else that's at least as important as that whole constitutional framework in determining what actually happens in the real world, and in particular what comes out of the judicial branch and court systems in the real world. The reality is, you can have the best laws in the world, the most elegant text, and the best Constitution. But at the end of the day, if you're not willing to put money into the institutions that actually carry out the work, the documents are capable of becoming empty. The promises are capable of being unfulfilled.

We can *say* that court systems are supposed to do any number of things. But if funding only allows them to be open three days out of the week, some of the things that on paper they are supposed to do probably will not get done.

Likewise, the management of resources within court systems is also really important, assuming that there is a question about whether the resources are adequate to do the job. To the extent that we're not able to use those resources as effectively as we would want to, then court systems are not going to be able to live up to the promises on paper that they are supposed to fulfill. That's the reason why I think institutional issues, court administration, governance, and funding are as important to understanding what actually happens in the real world, or at least are a major limiting factor on what happens in the real world, as is all the constitutional stuff. Even though the latter is what most of us came out of law school believing was really important in defining what the courts are and how they function.

So let's talk about accounting very briefly. Another quick show of hands: How many of you thought that accounting was one of your favorite classes in law school? None. Okay. *[Laughter from the audience.]* So I have found that if you are in a group of lawyers, and you want to [bore them], just start talking about accounting.

So accounting is boring for pretty much all of the reasons that most of you think that it is. But it is also profoundly important and interesting. So one way to define accounting is as the technology for capturing information relating to the financial status of institutions and the flows of money into and out of them. Good accounting is what allows us to achieve transparency and to know something about how much money is actually going in, and where it's being spent, and how.

When you have good accounting rules, one of the implications is that organizations that are spending money are also keeping track of it, in a way that makes this accessible to outsiders, to see what happened. Where was money spent and how? That's useful for a whole bunch of different reasons.

Here at RAND, as Paul Heaton was saying earlier, we're really interested in data, and in being able to do empirical research, and in trying to answer analytical questions about things like whether particular court system practices are more cost-effective or "better" than others. This exercise becomes much easier to do if you first have good data to work with. And accounting is one of the ways that you generate good, consistent, meaningful, reliable data, at least when it comes to the money side of the picture. This is true with regard to the courts and the judiciary, as it is with regard to lots of other kinds of institutions.

It turns out that accounting is also really important to any kind of an organization that wants to be able to make a case to the outside world about its resourcing levels. Say what you will about how accounting rules apply to the private sector and whether or not corporations play games with them. There is nevertheless an elaborate set of standards that dictate that certain kinds of information about finances are going to be disclosed. By virtue of these disclosures, people are going to know something about public companies. And as a result, they can hopefully make informed decisions about whether or not investments are wise and whether or not the companies are doing worthwhile things with the money that's been entrusted to them.

For state court systems, particularly in a time when austerity budgets in state governments are causing difficulties and heartburn, and where there is a case to be made that resourcing levels are not adequate, that budget cuts are having a really deleterious impact—being able to *document* how much money has come in, how it's been spent, where the cuts have had their impact, and why it is that reduced funding is a really problematic issue, in terms of its operational and institutional impact on the courts—being able to make that case in a clear, compelling way is very important from an advocacy point of view. Even beyond the fact that for those of us on the outside, we simply want to look at the data so that we can know the answer to some of those basic descriptive questions. If you want to be a court system advocate, being able to show the data, and to have people trust it, is key.

Accounting is important to those of us at RAND because we care about the data. And accounting is foundational to having data that is good enough so that we can then begin to do all the fancy analytical things that people at RAND like to do. But accounting is also important to court systems because it is foundational to their being able to make the case for what the funding levels really are and why it's problematic when the funding levels get cut. Here again, these are the kinds of arguments that we need to be able to make publicly so that there's greater public consciousness for why this stuff is important, and how. I think I will leave my introductory remarks there. Thanks again for joining us today!

CHAPTER TWO

Financing, Governance, and the "State" of State Courts

The initial panel discussion of the conference was moderated by Joseph Doherty, then director of the Empirical Research Group at UCLA School of Law. Participants on the panel included Chief Justice Lorie Skjerven Gildea of the Minnesota Supreme Court; Judge Carolyn Kuhl of the Los Angeles Superior Court; Mary McQueen, president of the National Center for State Courts; and Michael Greenberg, senior behavioral scientist and then director of the RAND Center for Corporate Ethics and Governance.

Joseph Doherty began the session by introducing the panelists, and he then posed a series of questions as a launching point for panelist discussion.

How Do Court System Funding Mechanisms Vary Across States, and How Have the Mechanisms Changed Due to the 2008 Financial Crisis?

In responding to the question, Greenberg began by noting that there are two major dimensions of variation in how state court systems are financed. The first dimension involves the potential for self-funding and the direct generation of revenues by the courts themselves. The second dimension involves the distinction between county-level and state-level funding for the courts. Greenberg suggested that the states vary widely in the degree to which county-level funding is important to maintaining the courts. He also observed that in the preceding decade, some larger states, including California and Florida, had moved in the direction of centralizing their funding of the courts at the state level.

McQueen then observed that about 32 states fund their court systems primarily at the state level, while the remaining 18 fund their court systems primarily at the county level. As a frame of reference, she also observed that state court expenditures represent only 1 to 2 percent of state general fund revenues, on average. She pointed out that the role of the courts is not to generate revenue and that most court-generated revenue actually reverts to the general funds of the states, rather than being dedicated to (and under the control of) the courts and judiciary.

Judge Kuhl then observed that dedicating fines-and-fees revenue to support the courts can actually have a budgetary downside. She described a recent supplemental allocation of $90 million to the state court system budget in California, drawing from fines-and-fees revenue. Unfortunately, a shortfall in fines and fees actually collected by the courts cut the supplemental funding that was available to the courts almost in half. Kuhl pointed out that there are serious negative consequences for courts in becoming dependent on fines and fees for revenue, as opposed to appropriations from the state's general fund, given that the courts have very little control over ups and downs in the fines and fees that they realize.

Both McQueen and Greenberg observed that similar problems arose in Florida following the foreclosure crisis, where the legislature put a special filing fee on foreclosure cases and gave that revenue to a trust fund dedicated to supporting the courts. The funding mechanism worked well during the temporary surge in foreclosure filings, but it then caused the courts to go into the red when foreclosures started to tail off several years later. McQueen and Greenberg also talked about the pros and cons of committed allocations from state general funds as an alternative mechanism for supporting the courts. Both observed that the successfulness of this mechanism can also become uncertain in budgetary hard times for the states and that it has worked better in some states than it has in others.

Kuhl and McQueen then briefly touched on some other subtleties relating to fines-and-fees revenue generated by the courts. Kuhl observed that reductions in fines and fees collected by the California courts may be resulting from several different factors, including reduced filings as a response to fee increases that were imposed by law, more litigants qualifying for fee waivers, or more people who simply can't get to court because of courthouse closures. Kuhl said that the judiciary simply doesn't have a handle on what the explanation is for the reduced collection of fines and fees. McQueen then observed that in California, other financing practices imposed by the state have magnified court system budgeting challenges faced by the court system. In particular, she observed that the use of a trust fund to "roll over" budget savings between time periods had historically allowed the courts some ability to normalize the ups and downs in available funding across revenue sources, but the legislature had swept those funds away from the court system during the height of the state's budget crisis.

Justice Gildea concluded by describing the state court system budget in Minnesota. She observed that the Minnesota courts are now state funded, after a 20-year transition from being county funded. The Minnesota courts receive about $300 million in annual funding from the state's general fund, which amounts to less than 2 percent of spending by the state. Justice Gildea observed that almost all of the funding of the courts in Minnesota is done through the state's general fund and is controlled by the legislature, and that fines-and-fees revenue collected by the courts is not controlled by the courts. Gildea said that she has framed the question of adequate funding for the court system as a public safety issue when talking with legislators about funding. She believes that this approach has been successful in Minnesota because citizen legislators appreciate the role of government in ensuring public safety.

What Is the Governance Structure of the Courts in Minnesota? Did This Help to Make the Courts More Resilient to Economic Conditions? And How Does the Minnesota System Compare with Governance Elsewhere?

Justice Gildea began the conversation by describing the Minnesota Judicial Council, which is the policy arm of the court system in Minnesota. She observed that when the state transitioned from county funding to state funding in 2005, the Chief Justice decided to share her governance authority over the courts by creating the Judicial Council, which is a 25-member body that sets policies for the branch. Fifteen of the members are trial court judges, and these include the chief judge of each of the state's trial court districts, the president of the trial court judges' union, and several slots for discretionary judge appointments by the Chief Justice. Six members of the Judicial Council are administrator members, rather than judges.

Gildea went on to describe the functions of the council, which meets monthly to set policies for the state court system, decide how much money to ask for from the legislature, and determine how to allocate resources across the court system. Gildea observed that the creation of the Judicial Council, with collaborative decisionmaking and direct participation by the people most affected by the council's budget decisions, has made Minnesota much more resilient in responding to the recent budget crisis. She then recounted the example of the Judicial Council reallocating resources to Rochester, Minnesota, based on data suggesting relative undercapacity and a shortage of judges there. Gildea said that the impact of this intervention in ameliorating case backlog in Rochester had been huge, and that the decision to do this involved other Minnesota districts giving up resources to help improve conditions in Rochester. She also suggested that the Judicial Council model of governance, which involved direct participation and buy-in from local judges and communities who were giving up resources, is what facilitated Minnesota's ability to carry out this decision.

Gildea also noted that the Judicial Council model of oversight allowed the state courts to centralize some of their administrative functions, thereby increasing efficiency. In that vein, the state has consolidated its network of court administrators, reducing their number from 87 (one based in every county) to 48 across the state.

Greenberg then interjected to ask what led Minnesota to adopt state-level control of the court system and whether this was driven by the belief that this would offer a better mechanism for apportioning resources. Gildea responded that formation of the council was driven by the Chief Justice's belief that a state-funded system also required a statewide framework for governing the system, beyond simply allowing the conference of chief judges to treat each trial court district as a separate fiefdom. She said that there was a need for statewide policymaking and resource allocation so that participatory decisions could be made based on the best interests of the state as a whole.

Discussion then shifted to address the court system governance models and choices of other states. McQueen described the governance systems in Oregon and Florida. In Oregon, she pointed out, the move to centralize funding for the courts by the state legislature actually originated at the county level. Recognition then followed that decisions about how to allocate the revenue would likewise need to shift to the state level. In Florida, by contrast, McQueen described a state constitutional discussion that began with an argument to consolidate the costs of the public-defender system and then evolved to a broader argument to consolidate funding for the judicial branch and court system. And once that broader consolidation was enacted, it then led to more than a decade of discussion about how the state would actually carry the funding model out and what the governance mechanism would be.

Judge Kuhl then spoke about the centralization of court system funding mechanisms in California as a way to reallocate resources and address some of the disparity across California's counties. Kuhl described the process for this as partly deriving from California's Judicial Council, but also from a committee made up of the presiding judges of the state's trial courts.

In turn, McQueen then described a national trend toward governance reform in state court systems, in part through the increasing prevalence of participatory processes that help to unify the oversight of resources across trial courts. McQueen observed that governance challenges for state court systems are complex and cannot be resolved purely through best practices in traditional public administrative governance, in part because the judiciary is made up of independent, constitutionally authorized, highly educated professionals. In this regard, McQueen observed that judicial governance shares some important similarities with the participatory governance of physicians in hospitals and of tenured professors in universities. In each case, inclusive governance models are important to facilitate the buy-in of those participating and the recognition that basic decisions about resource allocation are being made collectively and fairly. Ultimately, McQueen suggested that all of this is important to achieving financial and functional accountability for state court systems, both to those who work inside them and also to outside stakeholders, including the other branches of government and the citizenry.

Greenberg then offered a concluding thought on court system governance, by reference to Ohio. Greenberg observed that Ohio is a state with a very decentralized court system in which much of the funding for the system flows from the counties in a manner that is not well tracked or easily accounted for at the state level. Greenberg observed that that financing mechanism ties back to governance, since the flow of money also reflects who has decisionmaking authority over the money. Greenberg concluded that Ohio illustrates how complex the local budgeting and governance picture actually is in some states.

When Courts Face Budget Cuts, How Do They Implement These in Operations, and What Are the Risks of Nonrestoration in the Long Term?

Judge Kuhl responded to this question by offering a detailed summary of how the California court system, and the Los Angeles County trial courts in particular, have responded to the state's budgetary problems since 2002. She observed that the Los Angeles trial court had gone from having 58 courthouses in 2002 down to 38 in 2014. She also observed that courtroom staff had been cut by 25 percent over the same period. Kuhl described the operational implications and fallout from these cuts in detail.

During 2008–2014, Kuhl said that there was a $160 million reduction in funding to the Los Angeles Superior Court, without accounting for increasing employee benefit liabilities over the same time period. She described a series of operational responses to address the shortfall beginning in 2010, including a statewide decision to institute furloughs, eliminate clerical jobs, downsize the use of court reporters, undertake a "soft" hiring freeze, enact a voluntary separation program for commissioners, and (in 2012) close 10 percent of existing courtrooms across the state's trial court districts.

In 2013, the Los Angeles Superior Court still needed to undertake another $57-million reduction in operations, on top of what had already been done. Kuhl described the decision-making process as deliberate and as involving a triage effort to try to continue meeting the courts' constitutional and statutory obligations as much as possible. The decision was made to maintain access to justice in all litigation types and not to close the civil docket altogether. Likewise, the aim was to try to distribute resources fairly within each case type and not create situations where some judges would be overloaded while others would not have enough to do.

With these principles in mind, Kuhl described the additional cuts that were made in Los Angeles. Eight courthouses and 23 additional courtrooms were closed; all referees were let go; court reporters were eliminated for most civil proceedings; discretionary alternative dispute resolution (ADR) programs were eliminated; and a radical hub consolidation was done, along the lines of differential case management. By way of example, Kuhl observed that Los Angeles used to handle small claims matters in 26 locations and now does so in only five. And personal injury civil matters for the entire county have now been consolidated into the downtown location.

To summarize the impact on the system, Kuhl described morale, security, and geographic access challenges that have resulted from the resourcing cuts. She also described several functional measures suggesting impairments in the speed and volume of cases processed through the courts, including the observation that the number of open cases over two years in the general civil docket has tripled in connection with the cuts.

Kuhl concluded by observing that the aim for the future will be to preserve and enhance the function of the Los Angeles Superior Court as much as possible, consonant with the current budgetary reality. The Superior Court anticipates evaluating new technology solutions and case management practices that might harness additional efficiencies for the courts, as well as the trade-offs in geographic access and efficiency associated with such practices as hub courts, specialization, and differential case management.

What Are the Likely Long-Term Effects of Recent Rounds of Budget Cuts on State Courts?

McQueen began by observing that by 2013, court systems in many states had rebounded from the resourcing cuts they experienced at the height of the Great Recession, at least in part. However, significant cuts remain in many states, and particularly so in California. McQueen went on to say that looking forward, a key concern about court system budget cuts has less to do with continuing fiscal and revenue shortfalls within state governments and more to do with the potential for retaliation by legislatures and governors. McQueen identified several states where retaliatory efforts to cut court system resourcing have already occurred, based on politically unpopular decisions reached by the courts. Meanwhile, McQueen observed, another major problem is that the public does not recognize that accumulating case backlogs in the courts are related to inadequate resourcing. Rather, the public perception is that backlogs have more to do with antiquated procedures and related inefficiencies in the courts. Thus, McQueen argued, there is a strong need for state court systems to show that they are pursuing increased efficiency and cost-effectiveness in the way they operate. At the same time, though, she also observed that related innovations can sometimes be difficult for the courts to implement. McQueen particularly discussed problems associated with using technology to reduce the need for court reporter services and language interpreter services. In both cases, the potential for savings in California was opposed by the respective public employee unions. That opposition contributed to a political environment that actively blocked efforts by the system to manage its own resources more effectively.

In a different vein, McQueen observed that in some states, the court systems have faced additional budgetary challenges, either by virtue of needing to submit their budget proposals for the governor's approval prior to reaching the legislature (a practice akin to that of an executive branch agency) or else by being subject to detailed line-item appropriations that restrict the courts in shifting their funds in pursuit of greater efficiency. McQueen suggested that these sorts of procedural budgetary issues may be an enduring challenge for some state court systems, given the environments in which they operate and the way that the separation of powers has evolved. These issues may also exacerbate the risk of challenge to judicial independence and the use of the purse strings by other branches of government to retaliate against politically unpopular judicial decisions.

Justice Gildea suggested that one potential, long-standing impact of budget reductions to the courts could be reduced public confidence in the justice system, particularly as courthouses close and people experience long lines when trying to access the system. She suggested that reduced access and system resources can present a public safety issue, as when a strained court system results in the reversal of felony convictions for lack of ability to meet trial demand. Legislators need to be engaged in a difficult but constructive conversation around problems like this.

CHAPTER THREE

Constitutional Dimensions to the Funding of State Courts

The second panel discussion of the conference was moderated by Paul Heaton, then director of the RAND Institute for Civil Justice. Participants on the panel included Chief Judge Jonathan Lippman of the New York Court of Appeals; Donna Melby, a partner with Paul Hastings who serves on the California Judicial Council; and Robert Peck, president of the Center for Constitutional Litigation and chairman of the Board of Overseers for the RAND Institute for Civil Justice.

Paul Heaton launched the session by introducing the panelists, and he then posed a series of questions to the panelists on constitutional issues related to the funding of state courts.

When and How Are Constitutional Principles Implicated in the Funding of State Courts?

Chief Judge Lippman began by suggesting that at its heart, the issue is simply whether funding is sufficient to allow the courts to carry out their constitutionally mandated responsibilities. Several more-specific concerns can then spin out of that, including judicial independence, maintenance of due process, separation of powers, and timely access to trials.

Donna Melby then suggested a corollary question: At what point would we say that an impaired court system is no longer performing its constitutional functions, such that we would deem it unconstitutional? Is there some metric for gauging this threshold, and what response ought to follow when the threshold is crossed?

Robert Peck then spoke to the latter question and about the response of the courts themselves to funding shortfalls that putatively threatened their constitutional function. Peck observed that there has been a series of cases addressing the status of the courts as a co-equal branch of government and the underlying argument that the courts cannot be made entirely dependent on what the other branches of government are doing fiscally. Peck described a series of state supreme court cases in Pennsylvania, Massachusetts, and Mississippi along these lines. In each case, a reduction in resources to the courts imposed by another branch of government was challenged through litigation. And each case supported the intrinsic power of the courts to ensure the adequacy of their own funding, in the face of budgetary actions by other branches of government that impaired the function of the courts.

Has the Basic Funding and Constitutional Challenge to State Courts Changed in Recent Years?

Chief Judge Lippman suggested that the constitutional cases mentioned by Robert Peck did not fully capture the most recent set of resourcing problems faced by state court systems. Lippman observed that in the contemporary context of state-funded, unitary budget proposals and appropriations for an entire court system, the problem increasingly involves the courts getting a letter from the governor's office instructing the judiciary and courts to take a 2-percent cut, or 5-percent cut, or 30-percent cut in their annual budget. Constitutionally, the courts are supposed to be independent in their function, but they are also interdependent with the other branches of government as well. So how are the courts going to deal with the situation when externally imposed funding cuts really do impair their constitutional function?

Lippman then suggested that the most analogous case dealing with this problem arose in New York in 1991. At the time, the Chief Judge put in a budget request for an 8-percent increase in funding for the New York courts, and the governor then revised that proposal down to a 2-percent reduction in funding for the judiciary. A dispute followed, which turned on two constitutional arguments. The first argument involved a provision in the New York constitution that required the governor to pass the judiciary budget on to the legislature intact, which the governor had violated. The second argument involved the more fundamental question: At what point does a budget cut to the judiciary become so severe that the courts cannot carry out their constitutional mission? According to Lippman, the context of this dispute in 1991 was very political, and the case was eventually resolved through mediation and a settlement. Ultimately, the legislature decided that it would reduce the court's appropriation below the level at which it had been prior to 1991. This was a compromise result, but it generated lots of ill will and distrust between the branches of government in New York.

Lippman concluded that the New York experience in 1991 invites some basic questions about funding that apply to state court systems more broadly. At what point do budget cuts truly become a constitutional issue? And when should the courts escalate this into a direct confrontation with the other branches of government? Lippman noted that there were long-term pluses and minuses for the court system in New York in going to that extreme in 1991.

Is There a Basic Conflict of Interest in Judges Deciding the Constitutional Question of Whether Resourcing to State Courts Is Adequate?

Donna Melby asked whether a basic conflict of interest argument had ever come up in the context of a last-resort lawsuit over the constitutionality of funding cuts to a state's judicial branch. Peck responded that there are several empirical and political questions that tend to come up in any of these cases. The first, whether the budget is indeed constitutionally inadequate, depends on what the responsibilities of the courts actually are in a given state. The second question is, assuming that the budget is constitutionally inadequate, then what are the courts permitted or required to appropriate to themselves? The third question is the political question: Is it ever wise for the judiciary to pursue this strategy, even when facing crippling budget cuts?

Without speaking to the political question, Peck pointed out that in many states, courts have found no fundamental legal problem with exercising this kind of authority on their own behalf when it's necessary for the courts to continue to operate. But in California specifically, Peck acknowledged, there is a bar on the courts actually ordering an appropriation for themselves.

Lippman then pointed out that even in California, the courts do have the ability to conclude that the budget violates the constitution, without directly ordering an appropriation. Lippman told the story of a dispute in New York over judicial salaries, which culminated in a high court case that found a constitutional violation in the failure of the other branches of government to consider proposed salary increases on the merits. Even though the court had not specifically issued an order telling the legislature and governor what to do, the finding of a constitutional violation was enough to change the situation and, eventually, to resolve the problem.

Melby and Lippman then observed that part of the successful resolution of the dispute over judicial salaries in New York had to do with political support and goodwill toward the judicial branch on the part of the business community and the bar. Peck summarized this another way by emphasizing that public recognition of the importance of the courts, and of keeping them fully functional by keeping them fully funded, is often central in these kinds of disputes—and lack of public recognition is problematic.

Do Courts Risk Being Delegitimized When Challenging the Constitutionality of Budget Cuts Imposed by Other Branches of State Government?

Donna Melby suggested that litigation and constitutional challenge is an absolute last resort for the courts in dealing with episodes of funding crisis. But, in turn, that invites the question of what the alternative to a constitutional challenge would be. The answer, said Melby, is that the bar, the business community, and the public need to be mobilized and educated to recognize what the funding problem is and why the courts need help. Melby pointed out that this kind of outside support did mobilize in New York in the dispute over judicial salaries (previously discussed), but bar and business communities have been much slower to appreciate the post-2008 situation that the courts in California and other states have faced. Melby said that the Chief Justice in California had been extremely effective as a public advocate on behalf of the courts there, but that she could not play this role alone, and that the question now is how others can help to make the argument and to build the political coalition in support of the courts.

Peck responded that this kind of coalition-building is surely important, but sometimes it is a lawsuit or threat of lawsuit that helps to bring about that awareness. Peck pointed out that it is not only the judiciary itself that has standing to bring these lawsuits, but also the bar. And litigation initiated by the bar can help to lessen the fallout and the appearance of self-interest on the part of judges, since the bar is simply acting to ensure its right of access to the courts. Peck pointed out that the 1991 dispute in New York over the constitutionality of the court budget there was concurrently cited by the Chief Justice in Kansas during her negotiations with her own legislature over the judicial budget in that state. Peck suggested that this was an example of how constitutional litigation in one state led to increased awareness of the problems and to successful resolution without litigation in another state.

Judge Lippman then talked about other steps that the courts can take to make the public and the other branches of government more aware of the consequences of budget cuts. Describing the example of New York, Lippman talked about a more recent budget cut of $170 million to the court system there. How did the courts respond to the cut? They laid off 500 people. They started closing courthouses at 4:30 p.m., causing a lot of inconvenience to litigants. This got noticed by the newspapers and by the legislature. The courts made the decision to continue allocating money to legal aid for the poor, based on the belief that this was constitutionally imperative, even while staff were being laid off and services were cut in other ways. In essence, the courts responded to the funding cut by articulating constitutionally based priorities, making difficult choices with visible adverse impact on the public, and not flinching as the consequences became clear to the other branches of government. In doing so, the courts also demonstrated that judges were not simply "feathering their own nests" through these choices. Lippman said that the public and the legislature in New York saw and respected what the courts were doing. And gradually, money has been restored to the courts' budget in response.

What Role Can Empirical Data and Research Play in Constitutional Conversations About Courts and Their Funding?

In addressing this question, the panelists expressed a tension between several competing considerations. Peck suggested that if there were a way to analyze data to determine a constitutionally adequate budget for state courts, then that could be a powerful tool for public policy purposes. Melby added that accurate documenting of court system expenses and striving for efficiency in court operations are basic complements to this kind of empirical analysis.

Lippman cautioned, however, that there are limits to the reach of empirical analysis in this area, in that some decisions about how court system resources get spent may be constitutional and/or strategic, rather than purely being driven by efficiency and empiricism. Regarding the former, Lippman observed that questions about what is right and fair are sometimes fundamentally involved in resource allocation decisions within the courts, quite apart from considerations of operating efficiency based on data. Regarding the influence of strategy, Lippman observed that sometimes in the face of court system budget cuts, operating decisions are partly influenced by the question of "where is the pain going to get the most attention," so that the system can elicit the popular and budgetary support that it needs to continue functioning. By implication, sometimes the "right" response to a court system budgeting problem might not be to minimize its operating impact in the short to medium term.

Stepping back, Peck suggested that it may be difficult to value justice as this is embodied by the court system, based on any simple empirical metric of court system function. Several factors contribute to complexity in any empirical analysis along these lines, including shifting court system dockets, demands, and responsibilities over time.

Might the Impact of Budget Cuts on Personal Injury Cases in California Create a Fundamental Due Process and Equal Protection Problem?

A member of the audience observed that the burdens of the budget shortfall in California courts have fallen heavily on personal injury cases, such that delays and geographic problems in accessing the courts have become particularly burdensome in those cases. She raised the possibility that personal injury cases may be receiving lower-priority treatment within the system than commercial cases, and she asked whether this would be grounds for an equal protection or due process challenge.

Robert Peck responded that due process embraces the concept that justice delayed is justice denied; that access to the courts is supposed to be a fundamental right; and that the consequences to the public of a widespread deprivation of access to the courts for personal injury cases are serious. This said, Peck also observed that successfully making an equal protection challenge to the status quo and to the putatively "rational basis" for how personal injury cases are being processed by the court system in California is, nevertheless, difficult to do. In a related vein, Lippman observed that any such challenge would tend to pull in governance questions about who is making decisions within the court system about how to allocate resources and what the priorities embodied in those decisions are.

Lippman concluded that there is a tension in many states between the personal injury bar and the commercial bar and a perception of inequity in how court systems address these two categories of cases. He observed that there is a need for good governance and wise choices within the judiciary about how to use the budget that they actually have. And, Peck added, the bottom line on equal protection challenges is that one has to treat similarly situated people the same. But the question of who is similarly situated, with regard to the tension between personal injury and commercial cases, is not straightforward.

Should State Courts Respond to a Fundamentally Inadequate Budget by Simply Shutting Down Altogether for Part of the Year?

Another member of the audience asked whether any judiciaries had ever responded to the legislature: "Look, you've given us enough money for only 11 out of the 12 months this year. So this August, we're simply going to shut down all nonemergency functions." The question continued, if the U.S. Congress can shut down the government, why can't the judiciary shut down and make everyone feel the pain until needed money is given? Has this ever been considered?

Peck answered that because of the speedy-trial requirement under the Constitution, this kind of tactic is never adopted across the board, and criminal cases always continue. But many states have imposed moratoriums on jury trials, which he suggested is akin to a shutdown response. Lippman went on to say that a shutdown response is not only not unprecedented, but that it is almost a necessity when budget cuts become draconian. In those situations, Lippman said that the courts run through all the options presented by Judge Kuhl in the earlier session for saving money: furloughs, closing courts for a while, shutting down courtrooms, and so on. All of these steps for reducing costs involve tactical and equitable issues to resolve. Lippman concluded that in his view, judicial leadership often has a responsibility to think more carefully about how to save and manage dollars in a budgetary crisis situation instead of simply imposing a complete shutdown across the entirety of the state court system. But sometimes the budget may indeed reach a crisis point at which something more needs to be done beyond simply deciding where to allocate each dollar that is currently available. Those are the situations in which a constitutional issue may need to be addressed.

CHAPTER FOUR

Keynote Address: Tani G. Cantil-Sakauye, Chief Justice of California

California Chief Justice Tani G. Cantil-Sakauye gave a keynote address during the lunchtime session of the symposium. The keynote was conducted in an interview and question-and-answer format, as moderated by Mary-Christine (M.C.) Sungaila, then a partner at the Los Angeles firm of Snell & Wilmer, now a partner at Haynes and Boone, LLP. Sungaila posed a series of questions as a launching point for the Chief Justice's address.

Can You Provide an Overview of the Structure of the Judiciary in California?

Sungaila first asked California Chief Justice Cantil-Sakauye for a description of the structure of the court system in California. The Chief Justice responded that California's judiciary is unique by virtue of its size and complexity and that the state court system consists of five basic components: the supreme court, the six courts of appeal, the 58 trial courts, the State Bar (which falls under the administration of the supreme court), and the Judicial Council. She also emphasized that the judiciary is more than just its thousands of employees and millions of square feet of courtroom and office space. It is foremost a constitutional body, with the Judicial Council responsible for creating the rules and policies that govern the judicial branch.

Cantil-Sakauye continued, explaining that understanding the structure of the judiciary is essential to understanding the budget of the California state court system. The judiciary's budget is 1.4 percent of the state budget. The money first comes to the Judicial Council, then cascades down to the supreme court, then to the courts of appeal, then to the 58 trial courts, and, finally, to each court. Each court is responsible for its own budget and priorities and, over the last five years, how it implements budget cuts at the local level. Cantil-Sakauye emphasized that while the judiciary is a unified system, there is a lot of autonomy built into it at the local, trial court level.

Can You Describe the Transition from Local to State Funding of the Judiciary?

Sungaila followed up with a question about the transition from local to state funding of the California judiciary over time. Cantil-Sakauye responded that she thinks of the judiciary as being "17 years young" because the courts were unified 17 years ago. Trial courts, she explained, which used to be funded by the counties, became state funded, "for good or ill." By implication, when the state has money, then the courts have money; when the state does not have money, neither do the courts.

Sungaila followed up by asking why the judiciary has been disproportionately affected by state budget cuts. Cantil-Sakauye answered that she had not had any involvement with judicial branch financing until she joined the Judicial Council in 2008. Cantil-Sakauye explained that the judicial branch is almost entirely state funded. Throughout the recession, no one in state government knew whether the recession would continue to worsen or when it would end, so every year saw a series of ad hoc, worried reductions. Prior to the recession, the judicial branch had been managing its finances wisely, so it had money. In 2007–2008, the judiciary's budget was $3.7 billion. Since then, it has been reduced by $1.2 billion.

Cantil-Sakauye listed three main reasons for why the judiciary encountered such deep budget cuts. First, the state government was desperately looking for money, and every penny counted. Second, there was an effort to ensure that every state-funded entity was "functioning at its minimalist operation." The legislature knew that the trial courts had $550 million in reserves and, therefore, cut their budgets. The third reason is that the legislature is comprised almost entirely of non-lawyers, who often have to be reminded that the judiciary is vital to democracy and that laws are meaningless without the judiciary to interpret them.

Sungaila asked Cantil-Sakauye if her opinions about court budgeting had evolved since 2011. Cantil-Sakauye affirmed that they had. She explained that since becoming Chief Justice in 2011, she had faced constant requests from the governor to cut costs. Prior to 2011, Cantil-Sakauye believed in autonomy for the local courts, and she stated that she believes it even more strongly today. The judiciary survived the budget cuts, Cantil-Sakauye argued, because of the strong leaders at the trial court level who did what they needed to do to keep the courts going, and they were able to do so due to the autonomy they enjoyed.

Cantil-Sakauye said that her approach to advocacy for the court budget has changed. She realized that the governor and legislature have countless choices to make about each disposable dollar and that she must make the best case for why they should invest in the judicial branch. This takes time, education, and exposure to the courts. Now when she goes to the Capitol, Cantil-Sakauye does not assume that anyone there begins with *a priori* knowledge about the courts. Instead, she starts at the beginning and invites legislators to meet with her and to visit the courts and see them in action.

Finally, Cantil-Sakauye emphasized the need, more than ever, for a stable funding mechanism for the courts. She firmly believes that there will be another economic downturn in the next five to eight years, and that courts must be ready for it.

What Role Can Research and Data Play in Informing the Public About Court Budgetary Issues?

Sungaila asked Cantil-Sakauye about what role research can play in improving public discussion and civic education about court budget issues, as well as what data she wishes she had to support her advocacy efforts.

In answering the first question about the judicial branch's use of research, Cantil-Sakauye stressed the importance of data. She observed that "without objective evidence, you cannot win your argument." Cantil-Sakauye provided several examples of how data have driven changes in the judicial branch. Riverside County and San Bernardino County, known as the Inland

Empire, are the fastest-growing counties in California. They used data to drive a judge-workload assessment to determine how many more judicial officers were needed there. The legislature has been somewhat open-minded in response, authorizing more judges but not yet funding them.

Another groundbreaking use of data occurred two years ago in an effort to determine a different workload methodology for appropriating money. In the past, because counties funded trial courts, courts in wealthier areas had better funding. To address the disparity, the Judicial Council came up with a new assessment based on types of cases, and they were able to develop a more appropriate level of funding per county to equalize access to justice.

Cantil-Sakauye also outlined her "wish list" for data. She said she would like to be able to show the legislature the economic impact on businesses of courthouse and courtroom closures, as well as the economic impact of delaying civil business cases. In addition, Cantil-Sakauye noted that she would like more research to support what she knows is true: that much of the strife we see in the world can be attributed to the lack of rule of law.

What Is the Future of the Judicial Branch in California?

Sungaila noted that rule of law initiatives are common in the American Bar Association and through other auspices and that they are integral in the United States, not just abroad. She then asked Cantil-Sakauye about the broader, long-term future of the judicial branch. Cantil-Sakauye shared a term she coined to reflect her vision: "Access 3-D." The first element of three-dimensional access is remote access to the courts. Litigants should be able to file, search, and appear electronically for all appearances that do not require long evidentiary processes. The second dimension of Access 3-D is physical access. Cantil-Sakauye pointed out that residents of San Bernardino County, Riverside County, and rural counties have to drive three hours one way in order to get to court. The result is that they do not go to court. This is essentially a denial of justice by geographic inaccessibility. Cantil-Sakauye stressed that there need to be physical courthouses with enough staff to serve the population. The third element of Access 3-D is equal access, which includes appropriate support for self-help, corresponding waivers of fees and costs, aid to pro se litigants, and language access.

This vision is the prism through which Cantil-Sakauye sees all initiatives. She also discussed the Futures Commission, which was recently mentioned by Governor Jerry Brown in his budget. Cantil-Sakauye noted that she has brought in some of the governor's people to look at four areas of the state court system: (1) structural, statutory, and governance improvements to criminal and traffic court; (2) civil and small claims court; (3) family law, where 90 percent of litigants are pro se; and (4) administrative and fiscal governance structures. Cantil-Sakauye also pointed out that perhaps the branch needs a funding formula that includes a growth factor that kicks in automatically every year.

Is There a Role for Anecdotal Evidence in Advocating for Increased Funding for the Judiciary?

In her next question, Sungaila referred to her experience on charitable boards, where she said she had learned that the best way to raise money can be by discussing the needs of particular individuals and families, rather than structural needs for society as a whole. She asked if there might be similarities to the way that Cantil-Sakauye approaches funding discussions in the legislature.

Cantil-Sakauye answered that stories and anecdotes certainly have an impact. She recounted how three years ago the Judicial Council, following the model of the New York Judiciary, began holding hearings, asking individuals who had had trouble accessing the courts or receiving services in the courts to testify. These hearings were underwritten by the One Justice foundation, the California Chamber of Commerce, and the California Bar Association. Cantil-Saukuye told the audience that she had integrated some of these stories into her State of the Judiciary address. In addition, the Judicial Council regularly presents legislators with a snapshot of their own districts: how many judicial officers are employed, how many cases there are, where budgets have been cut, and how many people have been laid off. In those snapshots, the Judicial Council also tries to include anecdotal information to show the legislators what it really means when they underfund the judiciary in their own districts.

Is Progress Being Made on an Online Docket in California?

The first comment from the audience concerned the lack of an online docket in California. The participant suggested that the efficiencies from an online docket would result in meaningful budget savings to the court system and the state. Cantil-Sakauye agreed and further noted that the judiciary's greatest deficiencies were technological.

Cantil-Sakauye emphasized that while electronic access means different things in different counties, the trial courts have already made a mighty effort to bring their communities up to speed with modern technology. Cantil-Sakauye said that she believes that if there had not been a recession, the $550 million that the trial courts had in reserves would have been allocated to technology. That money was instead spent to keep courts open and to pay employees. Over the last five years, Cantil-Sakauye said, the judiciary's advances toward technology were thwarted because the judiciary simply did not have the money to pursue this.

Now, however, the judiciary is in a different place, and the courts are once again building and integrating new technology. Although the technology varies from county to county, Cantil-Sakauye said that some courts do have online dockets. The smaller courts are heading in that direction more quickly, but Cantil-Sakauye said that she believes that Los Angeles County, with the largest court system in the world, is headed there as well. She said that she thinks this endeavor needs to pick up speed, however, and this is among her primary goals for the remainder of her tenure on the Judicial Council.

Another audience member asked why the electronic docket is happening on a county-by-county basis, rather than across the state. Cantil-Sakauye answered that a statewide electronic docket had, in fact, been attempted. She explained that in 2002, the California Case Management System (CCMS) was begun. The idea was that every law enforcement agency, district attorney, Department of Corrections, and Highway Patrol, from Reading down to San Diego, could enter all their legal information electronically. A lawyer in Los Angeles could go online and find all the pleadings against his or her client. The development was intended to be open ended because the state wanted court users to help create the system. Judges, lawyers, court administrators, and court clerks were brought in. Many agencies supported the CCMS, and several counties agreed to pilot it. CCMS was eventually completed in 2011. It worked, but a significant amount of money had been spent on it, and it had been cited as wasteful. Several counties were prepared to implement it, but it would have taken millions of additional dollars to roll it out in 58 counties. Although independent audits noted that it would save millions in the long term, the legislature said that it could not "spend a dollar today to save five dollars tomorrow." In 2012, the Judicial Council ended the program. Today, when people ask why there is no statewide docket, Cantil-Sakauye points out that there had been one, but they simply could not afford to pay for it in 2012.

While the CCMS was, according to Cantil-Sakauye, "grand and majestic," the new approach is for every court to put together its own case management system. Everyone recognizes the efficiencies of remote access, and the courts are following a uniform set of guidelines and standards. The aim is for everyone to have e-filing, e-records, searchable databases, and document management. The vast majority of trial courts that have begun this reengineering have chosen a system from Tyler, which is also used in many other states. The goal is that Tyler will eventually connect the courts in some way. While the new approach is not grand, it works. It is a patchwork approach not only because of the autonomy of the trial courts, but also because the courts are not as wealthy as they were before the recession.

Is the Criticism Levied Against the Judicial Council Valid?

Another audience member asked about judges who have criticized the Judicial Council. He wondered if the criticism was correct that the Judicial Council was wasting money and whether Cantil-Sakauye saw them as more of a nuisance or as a real problem. In response, Cantil-Sakauye noted that there would never be unanimity among judges. In terms of the major issues, however, such as access to justice and funding, she acknowledged her shock at the dissent. The vast majority of judicial officers, she notes, support the work of the collective on the big issues. Cantil-Sakauye said that she believes that judges should be able to object and speak their minds but hopes that the dissent would be civil and respectful.

Can You Discuss the Trends in Case Filings?

An audience member voiced her concern with the decline in civil filings and the corresponding decline in fees collected, which affects not only the courts but also law libraries. The questioner wondered what the source of the decline was and if there was a visible pattern.

Cantil-Sakauye explained that the judiciary examines filings every three years, so they do not have all the relevant research yet to explain the drop in filings. The decline has indeed been precipitous, though, from 10 million three years ago to 7.5 million most recently. Both civil and criminal filings have declined.

As for criminal filing fees, Cantil-Sakauye explained that current thinking posits that law enforcement personnel were laid off during the recession, which led to fewer arrests and criminal reports and, ultimately, fewer filings.

In the civil justice arena, Cantil-Sakauye pointed out that attorneys agreed to a temporary increase in filing fees, which has since become an acceptable way to fund the judiciary. This is, however, a barrier to justice, and it likely explains the decline in filings. Cantil-Sakauye does not think that fee waivers are a major cause for the decline because litigants must meet rather strict standards for waiver.

Another audience member asked whether there had been an increase in pro se filings, which Cantil-Sakauye affirmed was the case. The numbers in California are consistent with the nationwide trend toward more self-represented litigants. Cantil-Sakauye noted that people lost their jobs during the recession, leading to an escalation of legal problems, but that these individuals could not afford counsel, so they had to represent themselves.

In the past, courts had self-help kiosks with bilingual volunteer staff and classes to walk people through filing their own divorces and small claims. With the recession, these self-help devices fell away. Not only was there an increase in pro se litigation, then, but there was also an increase in the time it took to resolve the cases. Cantil-Sakauye explained that pro se litigants often have to return to court day after day for reasons that include understaffed kiosks and incorrect paperwork. This impedes access to justice.

What Is Your Vision for Stable Funding of the Judiciary?

Another audience member asked Cantil-Sakauye to share and elaborate on her vision for a stable funding mechanism for the judiciary. Cantil-Sakauye said that the answer lies with a subcommittee of the Futures Commission that is looking at administrative stability. The subcommittee is analyzing how the judicial branch can be reorganized in terms of employees and technology to better utilize its funds. Cantil-Sakauye said she believes that the subcommittee can find efficiencies that do not sacrifice due process but also align with the expectations of parties and lawyers. E-access, for example, will require an initial investment but will save money in the long term. What is needed is a formula for how the judicial branch should be funded, with a growth factor for caseload and the population and a maintenance factor to keep technology current. The subcommittee will be open to the public so that people can submit ideas and together create a sustainable, durable solution.

Another audience member followed up with a question about how to ensure that technological advances will not adversely affect lawyers and litigants, noting the cost of such technologies as the CourtCall remote appearance system. Cantil-Sakauye acknowledged the possibility of adverse impact from such advances and affirmed that the judiciary cannot be improved on the backs of court users. She told the audience that there is a working group, consisting of presiding judges and court executive officers, looking at the proliferation of court fees to bring consistency, logic, and fairness to the process. Cantil-Sakauye noted that the variation in and proliferation of court fees from county to county violates the ideal of court unification and is something that the Judicial Council takes seriously.

How Can the Legal Profession Help the Judiciary?

To wrap up the keynote address, Sungaila asked Cantil-Sakauye what lawyers, judges, researchers, and professors could do to assist the judicial branch. Cantil-Sakauye answered that educating the public is essential. People do not understand the importance of the work performed by lawyers and judges in trying to implement the rule of law fairly and objectively. She recommended that everyone do a little outreach, perhaps directly to a friend in the legislature or their local rotary club or through an op-ed in the *Daily Journal*. Cantil-Sakauye offered that if each person in the legal profession helped spread the word about "the good work" done by the judicial branch, then the judiciary would not be at the bottom of the restoration list. The work of the judiciary, and of lawyers, in this regard, remains very important.

CHAPTER FIVE

Empirical Research on Resourcing to State Courts

The third panel discussion of the conference was moderated by Nicholas Pace, a senior researcher and attorney in the RAND Institute for Civil Justice. Participants on the panel included Tom Clarke, vice president for research and technology at the National Center for State Courts (NCSC); Ingrid Eagly, professor of law at UCLA; Herbert Kritzer, Marvin J. Sonosky Chair of Law and Public Policy at the University of Minnesota Law School; and Geoffrey McGovern, political scientist with the RAND Institute for Civil Justice.

Nick Pace launched the session by introducing the panelists and explained that the format of the session was different, in that each panelist was invited to speak for 15 to 20 minutes on his or her own empirical work or insights, broadly, as this related to the topic of state court resourcing. The presentations were followed by a brief question-and-answer session with the audience.

Thomas Clarke, Speaking on Empirical Work for the National Center for State Courts Regarding State Court System Resourcing

Thomas Clarke began by introducing himself as a research economist and a technologist, rather than as an attorney. He explained that his intent was to briefly summarize the empirical research that has been done on the economic impact of state courts and also to recreate the intellectual journey that NCSC undertook during 2009–2014 in attempting to help the courts with their funding crisis, by way of research and data.

To begin, Clarke observed that in the wake of the Great Recession there were several court-commissioned studies undertaken by economic consulting firms, which sought to quantify the economic impact of case delay and other similar effects on the broader economy. Clarke observed that these studies uniformly suffered from serious methodological problems, such that the findings were of questionable validity and substantially overstated the impact of the courts on the economy. As a result, NCSC set out to conduct economic impact studies of its own by partnering with interested academic economists from the universities.

Clarke recounted that NCSC then ran into another problem, which was that there were no economists who had previously done this kind of research from a microeconomic perspective. Clarke went on to describe the data challenges that NCSC had encountered in working with an academic partner to specify a microeconomic model on the impact of the economic downturn on civil cases. Clarke described NCSC's work on this kind of microeconomic model as still being in progress. He also noted in passing that some academic economists tend to want to assess the value of state courts in a way that focuses almost entirely on direct costs and benefits from the standpoint of litigants, thereby neglecting other noneconomic aspects of value that state courts may contribute through their function.

Clarke then described NCSC as turning to the more-limited objective of looking at incremental changes in the courts and how those changes influenced what the courts did from a cost-benefit point of view. He described the focus here as being at the program-evaluation level and more on the criminal side of the courts, in regard to specialized court diversion programs. Based on this research literature, NCSC has built some cost calculators that can be used by court advocates to compute potential savings associated with the adoption of similar programs under specified assumptions. Clarke observed that a similar empirical literature and set of cost calculators are also available for some aspects of courtroom technology adoption.

But, with this being said, Clarke noted that this kind of empirical approach has not really extended to the civil side of what state courts do because of a lack of equivalent programs, research studies, and empirical findings. Although there are some relevant programs on the civil side, such as mediation and differential case-flow management initiatives, Clarke observed that there has been little formal evaluation work done on these to quantify and validate their impact. Clarke went on to suggest that even in theory, their chief impact may have less to do with their economic effects than with their impact on rule of law. In turn, Clarke explained that the latter is a fuzzy concept with more than one definition and something that is very difficult to measure, despite lots of academic research on the topic. NCSC has done some work of its own to try to clarify the rule-of-law concept in support of future studies on state courts, but so far this work has not come to fruition. NCSC's latest efforts in this vein have focused on building an index of rule of law, which might help to support future comparative studies on the impact of state courts.

In a very different domain, NCSC has also been involved in studies on litigant costs for various forms of civil action in the courts, such as divorce, personal injury, and consumer debt. The basic finding is that these costs are very high and might indeed be pricing many people out of the market for using the courts for these types of cases. Clarke observed that this might be an important part of the explanation for why civil filings have been in decline across the United States in recent years.

Finally, Clarke concluded by summarizing the research literature on public expectations about the value of courts, which generally finds a wide discrepancy between what the courts actually cost to operate and what the public believes they ought to cost. Clarke went on to suggest that the research literature does not offer much support for some well-known strategies for trying to mobilize more funding support for the courts. In particular, he suggested that broad public education efforts and the argument that the courts "ought to have a special funding status" among government agencies have not been successful as strategies for protecting or enhancing court budgets. Instead, the research shows that the public tends to reward greater accountability and transparency in court system operations, as well as visible efforts by the courts to improve their own performance and effectiveness. Clarke also suggested that courts pursue the strategy of improving public trust and, consequently, support for their own funding by consistently enhancing the experience of members of the public through all of their varied contacts with the court system.

Ingrid Eagly, Speaking on Her Empirical Study of the Impact of Remote Adjudication Technology on Immigration Court Proceedings

Ingrid Eagly began by explaining that she would be sharing findings from a then-forthcoming empirical paper on the use of remote technology to adjudicate immigration cases.[1] She observed that this kind of research is relevant to a discussion of state courts, in part because state courts are likely to become increasingly reliant on remote technology to adjudicate cases in the service of cost-cutting efforts.

Eagly began by describing the basic concept of remote adjudication, which (in the immigration context) involves a detained litigant who appears at his or her court hearing remotely, as from a jail or detention center. The respondent appears remotely on a television screen, while the other participants (including his or her counsel) are present in the traditional courtroom. Eagly observed that this kind of remote adjudication setup is not new and actually originated in criminal courtrooms using a "video phone" during the 1970s. But use has been gradually expanding to other settings and many types of legal proceedings. Advocates assert that remote adjudication (by video-teleconference [VTC]) is a cost-saving measure that can make dockets more flexible and improve access to counsel in a manner that is functionally equivalent to in-person adjudication (i.e., without impact on outcomes). Critics, on the other hand, have argued that remote adjudication in the immigration context will bias judges to issue adverse decisions against immigrants. And this debate is taking place in the context of regulations allowing for VTC hearings in immigration cases, without any requirement to obtain the consent of respondents to the proceedings.

Eagly explained that her current research project involves trying to understand the impact of VTC proceedings in the immigration context and whether criticisms about bias really hold true in empirical data. Eagly observed that this particular issue is one for which there is good empirical data for conducting research: namely, on the outcomes of immigration cases and on whether VTC was used in particular cases. She went on to describe the data that she collected on immigration hearings in different cities and her observation of in-person and remote court proceedings in those settings.

In a nutshell description of her quantitative findings, Eagly observed that in an overall comparison of VTC and in-person proceedings, one does see statistically significant, worse outcomes from the perspective of the respondent when the case is assigned to a VTC courtroom. The question, however, is why? Eagly said that the data do not reflect meaningful differences in actual judicial decisionmaking when individuals present immigration claims (e.g., for asylum). Rather, the meaningful differences appear in every aspect of the litigants' engagement with the adversarial process in the context of VTC, as opposed to in-person courtrooms. In-person respondents are more likely to obtain counsel, more likely to apply for relief, and more likely to apply for voluntary departure, as compared with their VTC counterparts. Eagly observed that her data do not support the conventional critique of VTC as biasing judges against litigants. However, she also went on to describe her qualitative work to investigate the impact of remote adjudication on immigration respondents who are being held in remote locations and to assess why those persons may become disengaged from the process. She found several effects associated with VTC adjudication, including respondent perceptions of unfairness; disruptions of

---

[1]   Ingrid V. Eagly, "Remote Adjudication in Immigration," *Northwestern University Law Review*, Vol. 109, No. 4, 2015, pp. 933–1020 (http://scholarlycommons.law.northwestern.edu/cgi/viewcontent.cgi?article=1217&context=nulr).

litigant interaction with counsel and with the court; diminished public access to proceedings; and more complicated litigation and procedural dynamics, which very possibly operate to the detriment of the litigants.

Eagly concluded by observing that her research spotlights the broader questions of how cost-saving measures like VTC proceedings may impact litigant participation in the immigration courts, as well as the overall legitimacy of those courts. In turn, those findings in the immigration context may also have implications for the adoption of VTC technology as a cost-cutting measure in various state court settings and proceedings.

Geoffrey McGovern, Speaking on His Empirical Research on Court System Resourcing for the RAND Institute for Civil Justice

Geoffrey McGovern began by explaining how ICJ became involved in doing research on state court system resourcing in the wake of the 2008 financial crisis. He described an initial overview study that he conducted with Michael Greenberg aimed at broadly exploring the dimensions of the impact of the financial crisis on state courts, including such areas as securities litigation, resourcing for legal aid, and effects on the judiciary. Regarding the latter, several of the judges on ICJ's Board of Overseers expressed interest in seeing deeper empirical investigation into resourcing for the state courts, where the funding actually comes from, and how and where the money gets spent.

McGovern described that ICJ's subsequent research effort on this topic began with a review of the annual reports of state court systems themselves. ICJ found that it was sometimes difficult to reconcile the actual budget information disclosed by the courts with the narrative accounts that they offered to describe those budgets and their operating impact. As a result, McGovern explained that the next step for research involved digging into the process behind judicial financing and related governance processes in several selected states.

Part of what was learned through this effort simply involved the challenges facing any effort to compare governance and financing mechanisms, much less data, across state court systems. McGovern observed that this theme had already come up in bits and pieces in the earlier panel discussion in the conference. The pilot qualitative study that Greenberg and McGovern did looked specifically at the court systems in Utah, California, Massachusetts, Florida, and Ohio, with the states selected to maximize the variance in how their court systems are financed and organized. And the challenge of looking across these states began with the absence of any standard definition in what technically makes up the "court system" at the state level. In some states, this includes, for example, judicial retirement benefits, courthouse construction, and facilities maintenance. In others, it does not. By implication, any comparative work on court systems across states tends to involve apples-to-oranges comparisons, in ways that are not only impossible to eliminate but tricky even to pin down and describe through research.

Another basic dimension of variance across state court systems involves fines-and-fees revenue. Setting aside philosophical arguments about whether the direct funding of courts by fee revenue is constitutional or wise, the states do, in fact, differ in the degree to which the courts collect such revenue and the degree to which such revenue is dedicated back to the courts for their own use. McGovern described the collection of fee revenue by the Massachusetts court in particular, where a large fraction of collected fees is retained by the court system in support of its own operating budget. McGovern observed that an operational drawback to this financing mechanism occurs when the court fails to project correctly what its fines-and-fees revenue for the year will be, leading to a shortfall and deficit in the resources that it needs to operate for the year.

McGovern then briefly shifted to talk about the county- versus state-level dimension in state court system funding. He described the court system in Ohio as an extreme example of a county-financed system for which data on funding are very difficult to obtain, even by the state court system itself. Here, the implication was not only that the states vary in the degree to which their courts depend on county-level funding, but also that some of the county-level systems may make it very difficult to track what is being spent on the courts and by whom. McGovern went on to talk about court-system governance mechanisms across the states, including how they, in part, tend to reflect the way that the courts are financed but also how they make up another basic dimension of the variation across states.

McGovern concluded by framing some questions to motivate future empirical research on state courts. How has the reform movement from county financing to state financing played out across different states? Has it provided a more stable funding base in the states that have adopted it? What has the impact been on access to justice? What are the implications of remittances from judicial fees and fines to a state's general fund? Is funding for the courts more or less resilient for court systems in which a larger share of that revenue is retained by the courts? And how much is a closed courthouse actually worth, in terms of its impact on, for example, Los Angeles or the state of California? He closed by sharing that it was a difficult task to try to address these kinds of questions empirically but one well worth the effort in terms of helping the states to operate more effectively and to fund the courts.

Herbert Kritzer, Sharing Some Reflections About Empirical Research on Courts

Herbert Kritzer began by suggesting that the fundamental question is to identify any negative consequences attributable to inadequate funding of the courts. He pointed out that this presents some design challenges for doing good empirical research, as well as the problem that some basic intuitions about consequences may be disproven by research.

By way of example, Kritzer described the empirical findings on plea bargaining. Kritzer suggested that a standard intuition about plea bargaining is that the frequency of this practice is sensitive to resource constraints and the pressure to resolve cases quickly when criminal caseloads are heavy. But notwithstanding that intuition, Kritzer explained that several empirical studies have shown that the proportion of guilty pleas across high-volume urban courts and low-volume rural courts actually shows little or no difference—an empirical result that contradicts a basic intuition about the impact of resource scarcity in the courts. Kritzer offered another example involving the intuition that scarce court resources would slow the pace at which cases are handled. Here again, he described multiple empirical studies that failed to confirm the intuition and instead suggested that other factors were more explanatory, ranging from local legal culture to differences in the complexity of the caseload being handled. Kritzer then pointed out a third example, with regard to an earlier comment that Judge Kuhl had made about the Los Angeles Superior Court adopting a master calendar in managing civil cases. Kritzer said that past empirical research on this issue found that the use by courts of a master calendar was actually associated with increased delay in case processing, rather than with improved efficiency. He concluded that these examples suggest that basic intuitions about the impact of court practices and resourcing can sometimes be wrong. And solid empirical research may be needed to assess whether the intuitions correspond to what is actually happening.

Kritzer finished by talking about some of the reasons why empirical research on courts and litigation is difficult to conduct and to interpret across studies. One problem that he pointed out is the difficulty in simply designating a unit of observation, like a "case" or a "trial." These terms can mean different things to different court systems, and, in turn, those meanings will result in different kinds of data being generated and collected by those systems. A similar problem can arise in empirical studies of case filing rates, based on different definitions and rules across states in what constitutes a filing and what the trigger criterion is for initiating a filing. Finally, Kritzer described his own efforts to look empirically at trial rates across states and discovering not only basic data challenges but also differences in substance and procedure that appeared to have a substantial impact on the number of trials. He suggested that in light of problems like this, empirical research on the courts requires an awareness of the deep, technical complexity of the institutions and processes that are being studied.

Q&A from the Audience

The question-and-answer session with the audience touched on several issues. One involved the question about how best to think about the costs and benefits of the courts, given that some of the value they generate is nonmonetary. The panelists noted that NCSC has done work to develop a standard set of court system performance measures, most of which are nonmonetary, for precisely the reason that the function of the courts cannot be understood purely in terms of cost efficiency. Another panelist observed that the trade-off between monetary and nonmonetary values in the function of the courts is arguably embedded in the Sixth Amendment to the Constitution, which requires access to jury trials for criminal cases but not civil cases. This provision was interpreted as a form of rationing, with regard to the nonmonetary values connected to the jury trial process.

Another set of audience questions pertained to Ingrid Eagly's work on immigration courts. One person asked whether the disparity in outcomes connected to VTC proceedings could be mitigated by more attorney or judge training or through other policy interventions. Eagly responded that there may indeed be policy reforms that could at least help to address the disparity and that this is an issue that she is actively thinking about. A second person asked what the implications of her basic findings are with regard to the future use of VTC in the courts. Eagly said that VTC adjudication is unlikely to go away in courts that have already adopted it, and, therefore, the question of how the technology can be used better and more fairly becomes very important.

Herbert Kritzer was asked whether the empirical definition for counting "trials" ought to be expanded to include various nonjudicial, administrative dispute resolution schemes. Kritzer agreed with the premise of the question and observed that the vast majority of trial-like proceedings and adjudications are happening outside the court system, as in the context of unemployment proceedings, Social Security proceedings, and the like. In context, Kritzer also pointed out that, properly construed, the state courts really are broader than just the judicial branch and may include various administrative bodies that are carrying out equivalent functions in specialized contexts, such as tax and workers' compensation.

A final question from the audience was whether it was feasible to parse the economic impact of delayed court proceedings at the level of individuals and businesses that go bankrupt or suffer other adverse consequences as a result of the delays. Thomas Clarke responded that studies that focus at the individual level, or even anecdotes that relate to the impact and cost on an individual level, may well be more effective as an advocacy tool on behalf of the courts, as compared with the attempt to study the economic impact of the courts in the aggregate. But the basic problem for any empirical research along these lines, Clarke suggested, is one of basic resource limitations. In contrast with studies looking at the individual returns on higher education, where, Clarke pointed out, there is a natural funding constituency to support that work, the courts are in a much less favorable position in funding similar research. In a related vein, Clarke observed that much of the work of NCSC has focused simply on trying to address the basic data problems in describing the performance of courts, and that it is incredibly expensive and difficult just to deal with that step, let alone reaching the economic impact question posed by the audience member.

CHAPTER SIX

Access to Justice and Business-to-Business Litigation

The fourth panel discussion of the conference was moderated by Geoffrey McGovern, a political scientist and attorney with ICJ. Participants on the panel included Craig Holden, partner with the law firm of Lewis Brisbois Bisgaard and Smith LLP, chair of the firm's national commercial litigation practice, and president of the State Bar of California (2014–2015); Rebecca Sandefur, associate professor of sociology and law at the College of Law, University of Illinois Urbana-Champaign; and Jeff Kichaven, founder of Jeff Kichaven Commercial Litigation.

McGovern launched the session by introducing the panelists and inviting each to respond to a brief opening question on the topic of access to justice and business-to-business (B2B) litigation. McGovern then invited questions from the audience for the panel as a launching pad for further discussion.

Question from Moderator to Craig Holden: In Your View, How Has the Business Community in California Been Affected by the Funding Crisis That the Courts Are Facing?

Holden commended the court leadership for doing as much as they can under difficult circumstances and noted that the funding crisis has affected businesses differently. In the context of a legal dispute, he observed that larger businesses are sometimes in a better position to tolerate the delays associated with diminished access to the courts, as compared with smaller companies and entrepreneurial start-ups that have fewer resources. He noted that some suggest that a defendant gains an advantage by the court delays because the plaintiff seeking to redress an alleged wrong is delayed in getting resolution, but he noted that defendants are affected because they also want to clear their names as efficiently as possible. Holden noted that anecdotal stories have spread about harm experienced by California businesses in the wake of court closures and reduced access. He offered the example of a business being unable to adequately protect its intellectual property rights as a result of delayed or diminished access to the courts, with the interim result of greater litigation risk and uncertainty and the potential for a bottom-line impact on the operations of the company and on how well it does. As another example, Holden described a recent business case that he had worked on that had been ready for trial, with continuances subsequently imposed four times not at the request of the parties, but by the court itself. Taken in the aggregate across the entire business sector, Holden surmised that similar delays and lack of access to justice could have an impact on the business climate and economy in the state if businesses were to lose confidence in the ability of courts to efficiently resolve business disputes. Businesses could decide that going to court is not the best way to resolve a dispute if the delays are too great. In addition, if other state jurisdictions offer more efficient judicial systems, it could be a factor in where businesses decide to locate themselves or litigate. In this vein, Holden touched on recent efforts by the state of Texas advertising in California to encourage businesses to relocate out of California, and he suggested that lack of dependable access to the courts could have a meaningful impact on the response of such businesses to such pitches.

Finally, Holden touched on the spending priorities of the courts in a time of austerity and the extent to which the courts have been sensitive to the needs of the business community. He suggested that more companies are turning to complex litigation courts for help when they have complex matters and that those courts may be better suited than the general civil courts to deal with the needs and challenges that businesses have, particularly in resolving complex cases in an efficient manner. In sum, Holden opined that there is a need for stronger funding by the legislature to the courts overall, including the complex litigation courts, to improve the timeliness of access to justice for business cases.

Question from Moderator to Rebecca Sandefur: Based on Your Research, How Has the Financial Crisis Affected the Cases Being Brought in the Courts?

Sandefur opened by providing a perspective on access to justice in the courts, based on recent survey findings about ordinary people from a midsized Midwestern city. When survey respondents were asked about their experience of potentially justiciable events during the preceding 18 months, about two-thirds of them reported at least one such event—a response rate that Sandefur described as being substantially higher than that reflected in national surveys from 20 or 30 years ago. Sandefur said that this finding reflects the reality that economic downturns are engines of civil justice problems, because downturns lead to things like people losing their jobs, being unable to pay bills, and losing their homes. Sandefur also observed that the vast majority of this activity never makes it into court because people handle it on their own in some way. She described the cases that actually make it to court as being like the visible part of an iceberg, such that most of the iceberg remains invisible below the surface.

Sandefur went on to describe how most people resolve disputes without the help of the courts. First, many people attempt self-help in these situations, as by direct negotiation with the opposing party. And when people look for outside help in connection with some kind of justiciable problem, they frequently do so through their own immediate social networks. Based on the latest survey findings, Sandefur said that only about one such problem in five leads a person to seek help outside of her or his immediate social network, and even in most of those instances, help is sought not from lawyers or the courts, but instead from other third-party organizations and agencies. Only 8 percent of the problems reported in Sandefur's survey sample had any kind of court involvement. By implication, the incidents involving courts represent only a tiny portion of the civil justice experience of the public. Sandefur went on to explain that the cases actually winding up in the courts mainly consist of family problems like divorce, which can only be resolved through court intervention, or of problems that involve somebody else's legal action, as when one becomes the object of somebody else's eviction or foreclosure proceeding. And, according to the survey results, in fewer than half of those situations did the survey respondent engage in any kind of advisory contact with an attorney.

Sandefur suggested that these dynamics create two basic problems for the courts. First, there are high rates of default in civil matters, simply because people do not realize that they are supposed to show up and do not understand the kind of matters that they are involved in. Second, the lack of understanding and familiarity with the process puts a high demand on the courts, in terms of dealing with people who have no idea where to go at the courthouse, what they are supposed to do, or how to interact with the system. Thus, one of the basic challenges faced by the courts is how to deal with legally unsophisticated people and to do so both efficiently and fairly. In concluding, Sandefur observed that one operating implication of austerity budget cuts to the courts can involve less self-help assistance to people like these, more "referrals fatigue," and more people who eventually give up on the system and wind up in default. When asked about substantive reforms that might help to address these problems, Sandefur spoke about the possible model of ombudsman programs in other countries, which seek to resolve disputes more cheaply and quickly than the courts typically do.

Question from Moderator to Jeff Kichaven: What Are Your Thoughts About the Alternatives to Court-Based Adjudicatory Processes?

In his remarks, Kichaven focused on making the argument that all court-connected mediation programs should be abolished. He observed that all such programs involve opportunity costs, given limited court system budgets. And he also argued that such programs have zero utility because the private marketplace handles the need for mediation services remarkably well. Kichaven went on to debunk a series of counterarguments in support of court-connected mediation services in civil cases. Of the argument that people simply will not mediate without court involvement, Kichaven pointed out that this has been disproven by actual experience, as in Los Angeles County in 2014 following discontinuation by the Superior Court of its own ADR mediation program. Of the argument that members of the public might not be able to find good mediators, Kichaven suggested that there is plenty of public information about mediation services available and that a simple smartphone search can easily locate qualified mediators. Regarding the question of affordable access to mediation, Kichaven pointed out that the marketplace includes mediators working at a wide variety of price points and that pro bono mediation services are available through the marketplace as well.

Kichaven then turned to address several other problems connected to mediation. He argued that access to high-quality mediation is better served by the private market than by state court mediation panels because the minimum qualifications for serving on court panels are low. He then addressed the problem of lack of diversity in the field of mediation, which he explained as resulting in large part from the difficulties for young people trying to break into the field. In turn, he described those difficulties as being exacerbated by submarket rates for entry-level mediation services, as these have been established by the state court mediation panels. Again, his conclusion was that if the court panels ceased to exist and the marketplace could speak instead, then the simpler cases would allow new mediators to be fairly compensated and to take the flexible time they need to break into the field. Kichaven summed up by saying that there is no need for court-annexed mediation programs to obtain a thriving market for mediation services and a thriving mediation community.

Q&A from the Audience

The question-and-answer session with the audience touched on a number of issues. The first set of questions dealt with mediation. One audience member asked which kinds of people are qualified to start as new mediators. Jeff Kichaven responded that many different people enter into the field of mediation, ranging from new law school graduates to experienced lawyers and judges to persons outside the legal profession who nevertheless possess relevant industry experience. He suggested that it is not necessary to be a lawyer to be effective as a mediator, although those starting from other professions tend to learn a lot of law to be competitive. Another audience member asked whether court-supported mediation programs were useful in opening new market opportunities for mediation services where these have not previously existed. Kichaven acknowledged that the court-supported programs might offer some value in this situation. However, he also cautioned against the potential drawback to litigants of depending on mediators whose primary responsibility is to serve the courts and to reduce the burden on courts.

In a related vein, a member of the audience asked what the rate of settlement of cases actually is for court-connected mediation programs that operate in California. Craig Holden responded that in his view and experience, the court-based mediation program in Santa Monica had been tremendously successful and that the judges have done a wonderful job in resolving a large percentage of garden-variety litigation arising from the business and consumer communities. Holden also said that as state bar president, he had heard accolades concerning other court-based mediation programs. Kichaven countered, though, that the opportunity costs to the courts are high and that, given limited resources and the core function of adjudicating claims, it would make more sense for the courts to focus their efforts on adjudication.

Moving to a different topic, another audience member posed a question to Sandefur, asking her about the importance of the 92 percent of justiciable problems reported in her survey that nevertheless did not generate any court system involvement. The audience member asked whether the courts should be concerned about the 92 percent. Sandefur responded that courts indeed ought to be concerned, in part because some of the 92 percent are being treated unlawfully and unfairly without their knowing it, which presents a rule-of-law concern. Sandefur also pointed out that the 92 percent of unfiled cases are entirely outside the surveillance of the courts, which is problematic for them in simply understanding what is going on. The audience next asked whether Sandefur had asked her survey respondents why they did not file or seek court involvement in all of these cases. Sandefur explained that in most such instances, the survey respondents indicated that they had never even thought about the courts and that they tended to think of most of these situations as being something other than a legal problem. Sandefur concluded that the most effective way to try to expand court involvement would likely involve educating or assisting people immediately at the point when they most needed that help, in the context of their personal problems. She also suggested that an inexpensive version of the intervention could be a simple sheet of paper explaining what was happening and what the person needed to do in context. More expensive interventions could involve phone contact and support to the person, but Sandefur acknowledged that the obvious drawback is that this practice is more expensive to carry out.

The panel discussion concluded with an audience request for a discussion concerning an innovative divorce website in the Netherlands, designed to address the unmet civil legal needs problem. Sandefur described the web portal as an attempt by the government to automate some of the processes and advice needed to navigate the divorce process and thereby achieve greater efficiency in legal aid. If the spouses cannot fully resolve their differences online, the system also helps to automate the process of choosing and hiring a mediator. Sandefur explained that the automated system goes all the way to generating the divorce decree for review and approval by a judicial officer. She also observed that the system helps solve a self-help problem that California encountered with uncontested divorces, which was that people failed to submit their divorce paperwork once completed and then incorrectly assumed that they were divorced when, in fact, they were not. Sandefur concluded that the Dutch divorce web portal is an example of using automation to handle a process that (in simple cases) does not require a lot of human judgment and to move people through that process quickly and in a manner with which they are okay. Kichaven also pointed out that similar systems are being developed in Europe to handle other categories of civil matters beyond divorce.

CHAPTER SEVEN

Final Keynote Address

The concluding address of the conference was given by William T. Robinson III, member of the law firm Frost Brown Todd LLC, co-chair of the American Bar Association (ABA) Task Force on Preservation of the Justice System, and former president of the ABA.

Closing Address of William T. Robinson III

It's now 4:15 in the afternoon, and I can't count the number of these programs that I've been to in the last five or six years. And I have taken ten pages of notes today. To me at least, that says a lot about the substance and the quality of this program. And I want to begin by expressing my respect and appreciation for all those who put the work into this: Paul Heaton, Robert Peck, everyone who worked so hard on this.

This is really an important day in the cause for courts to be adequately funded. I suspect there's no one here who can identify a court system in this country that is overfunded or a judge in a system in this country who is overpaid. I don't think that is a situation that we have to worry about. Not when the New York courts right now rank at the top in terms of percentage of their annual overall state budget allocated to the courts in the amount of 4.6 percent, and the tragedy of California when it comes to funding courts as we heard today from the chief justice is at 1.4 percent. Not when more than 20 states are receiving under 2 percent of their overall state budgets, and what little progress we have made in the funding of our court systems since coming out of this most recent recession is not enough progress.

And it's not enough for any of us to be satisfied or content with the situation faced by the American judiciary in the 50 states in this country. It's an honor for me to be on this program; it really is. I'm basically a country lawyer from Kentucky. I'm not a scholar. I haven't done the research that so many of you have done. But I became passionate about the issue of the underfunding of the courts four or five years ago as I was moving up into the leadership with the American Bar Association, because it seemed to me then and it seems to me now that as officers of the court, as citizens of this great country, there is no cause that merits our commitment and support more than the funding of our courts. As Tom said earlier, courts are about—and I wrote this down exactly because I was so impressed with it, Tom—you said courts are about a lot more than cost. Courts are the cornerstone of our American constitutional government. Courts are the key to the quality of life that we have in this country. Courts are what make American democracy tick. Courts are who we are. I mean, it's just the essence of our freedom.

But as we were kidding earlier, I think during the lunch break several of us [said], when's the last time you went to a cocktail party and somebody came up to you and said, "Let's talk about the courts"? Can anybody remember that happening? I can't. It's not something that people have on their minds unless something negative has happened in their family, with a grandchild, with a niece, with a neighbor. It typically is not an experience that's treasured in the family lore for having been a high point of their family experience. It just isn't.

And most people have no idea what the courts do. Most legislators, as we heard again today and were reminded today, are no longer lawyers. Legislatures don't include lawyers like they did at one time in the history of this country, and so even the legislators need to be educated about our courts. The chief justice of Minnesota, Chief Justice Gildea, said her approach is to talk about public safety, and she's had success with that in Minnesota because, as citizen legislators, her legislature can understand, and it apparently has an emotional impact on them. Chief Justice Sakauye said, "Educate the public." That's the charge she gave us today: "Educate the public." And that's what we really need to do. But even as lawyers, how many of us are actually doing that? How much allocation of our personal time, intellect, resources do we allocate to the courts, and is it ever really enough?

When Joanie and I had the privilege of leading the ABA, we traveled to over 60 cities, spoke to the media, spoke to law schools, spoke to student bodies, spoke to faculty; I always tried to find a way to weave the subject of the courts into whatever discussion I had the privilege of leading or participating in. I always tried to bring it around to the courts, and I never received any backlash for that. I never had anyone show any resistance or rejection of that. In fact, most of the time, the response that I got was along the lines of "I've never really thought about that; I've never really considered that." And it caused people to stop and take time to consider that the very framework of our society is at stake when it comes to our courts being underfunded.

The ABA woke up to this problem approximately five years ago. Steve Zack—who's a very close friend of mine, as many of you know—he and I were coming up on this adventure to run for president-elect and be president of the ABA. And what had been the tradition in the ABA for much too long, at least in our opinion, was that each president had his or her project for that year that was going to save at least Western civilization and maybe the rest of the world. And then the next year it was a new program, and we kept rolling over these programs and spending this money. And Steve and I decided we should take on a cause that had historical significance and merited continuity of leadership. We wouldn't worry about who got the credit. We would be focused on the opportunity to serve and to make a difference over a period of time. And we chose the courts as our cause and established in his year as president the task force on the preservation of the justice system.

We were successful in getting his partner David Boies and Ted Olson—a Democrat, a Republican, a bipartisan approach—to spend two years on this. And you all recognize those names, I'm sure. You know how busy they are. You know the demands on their time. You know the kind of fees they charge because they are so excellent at what they do. But they gave us two years of their time and with the expertise of Mary McQueen and the National Center for State Courts, we set out on a task over a two-year period with Ted and David's leadership and their drawing power to have regional programs held all over the country to take testimony, to get anecdotal information, to go from area of the country to area of the country, to get people to think about this issue. Did we turn the world upside down? I doubt it. But I do think that we got the attention of the public community, the legislative community, the governmental community. I do think that we got the media to pay attention. At least we got editorial support all around the country.

During that period of time, I saw as much editorial content and attention to the courts as I guess I've seen at any time in my career. And it was very satisfying for us to make that progress. But progress is not perfection. Progress is not anywhere near where we need to get in terms of improving the situation when it comes to our courts. I'm fascinated with the studies, I'm fascinated with the data, especially to the extent that the data can be used as a tool to be more effective in persuading government and the public at large to respect, appreciate, and more adequately fund our courts. But I am really convinced that, along the lines of what the chief justices told us today, that it's really more about communication, getting more people to understand and recognize that the courts are essential—essential—to our government and our American way of life. I'll take these notes with me. I'll continue to go to these seminars. I'll continue to learn.

But I really do believe that, as we had the chief justices here today—and I haven't figured out yet how to achieve this; it's a delicate challenge for someone like myself, who's a litigator, to say this to judges—but I still am convinced with all the work we've done on this issue over the last four or five years, with everything that we've learned, I'm still convinced that the best communicators about the court systems in our country are the judges. I truly believe they have the most knowledge, the most experience, the most perspective; and yet, for whatever reason, it remains one of our biggest challenges to figure out how to get our judges out into the communities. In politics we say, "Make friends before you need them." And I get the calls from the court and I get the pitch about we have to get it to the legislature when there's an issue, when there's a funding crisis, when there's a problem. And most of us who work around government recognize that that's not really the best way to do it. The best way to do it is to interact with the legislature, build relationships, get on a first-name basis, bombard them continuously with additional information, provide them with the kind of anecdotal information that gets inside their person, not just inside their intellect, so that they're really caring about this issue that's so important to everyone and certainly important to us.

But it doesn't seem to happen. It doesn't seem to happen. I've tried it at home. I've tried it on a state level. I've tried it with the Judicial Division. Of course, those active in the Judicial Division are doing it or they wouldn't be there in the first place. But I've talked to them about it, and I just don't understand why, and I don't know how the challenge is going to be solved, as far as getting more judges. They do it at election time in those—what is it—26, 28 states where election of judges is still going to be the way judges are selected. They're out there for the campaigns. But once the campaign's over, they don't really see it. And I think we need citizens, we need lawyers, we need judges; we need a full-court press on this issue. And it's not for sprinters. This is for marathoners. The reality of this is we've got to be in this for the long haul, and we can never be satisfied with what little progress we're making because there are just so many people out there without access to the courts, without money for lawyers, without even the opportunity to take advantage of what our excellent court systems have to offer. I know that everyone agrees with this.

I just feel like at the end of a day like today, we ought to end on a high note. We ought to come out of here with the enthusiasm that brought us here. We share a commitment to something that is probably as professionally important as anything we have on our list of priorities. To sit and still hear that courthouses are closed, after working on this for over five years, to hear that more courtrooms have had to be closed, that's just too painful to really accept, and yet it's the reality of our situation. We leave here today with the question, okay, what are we going to do about it, and how are we going to improve the situation? Courthouses must be open for small business. Courthouses must be open for families that are in crisis. Courthouses must be open to keep the public peace and tranquility. Courthouses must be open for the wheels of justice to turn.

We're committed. We need to be more missionary-like, I respectfully submit, and enlist more of our sisters and brothers to join us. The organized bar, you would think I'd come from this angle because it's been such a big part of my life, but I'm very proud and grateful for what the organized bar has done nationally at least in the last five or six years. But I keep emphasizing that it's not nearly enough, and it hasn't gotten us close enough at all to the goals to which we have to remain very committed. Ours is absolutely the most unique constitutional democracy in the history of the world. I mean that is just inarguable, inarguable. Our constitutional democracy is the key to what? Our freedom. Our freedom. And the courts are essential to our enjoying and protecting that freedom, not only for ourselves, for our children; but now at my age, all I think about most of the time are my grandchildren and how important it is for them. So I'll finish on that note that was the key in Law Day in 2012, when I was privileged to be president of the ABA. No courts, no justice, no freedom. Thank you all very much.

Conference Agenda

UCLA-RAND Center for Law and Public Policy

presents

Discount Justice: State Court Budgeting in an Era of Fiscal Austerity

RAND Corporation
1776 Main Street, Santa Monica, CA 90407

January 12, 2015

Meeting Agenda

8:00 a.m.   **Registration**

8:30 a.m.   **Welcome**
Paul Heaton, Director, RAND Institute for Civil Justice
Laura Gómez, Vice Dean, UCLA School of Law

8:45 a.m.   **Introductory Remarks**
Michael Greenberg, RAND Corporation
Joseph Doherty, UCLA School of Law

9:00 a.m.   **Panel #1:** Financing, Governance, and the "State" of State Courts

Moderator: Joseph Doherty

- Michael Greenberg
- Judge Carolyn Kuhl, Los Angeles Superior Court
- Mary McQueen, National Center for State Courts
- Chief Justice Lorie Skjerven Gildea, Minnesota Supreme Court

10:20 a.m. **Break**

10:40 a.m. **Panel #2:** Constitutional Dimensions to the Funding of State Courts

Moderator: Adam Winkler, UCLA School of Law

- Robert Peck, Center for Constitutional Litigation
- Chief Judge Jonathan Lippman, New York State Courts
- Donna Melby, Paul Hastings

1

12 noon   **Lunch and Keynote Address**

Tani G. Cantil-Sakauye, Chief Justice of California

Moderated discussion by M.C. Sungaila, Snell & Wilmer

1:30 p.m.   **Panel #3:** Empirical Research on Resourcing to State Courts

Moderator: Paul Heaton

- Thomas M. Clarke, National Center for State Courts
- Ingrid Eagly, UCLA School of Law
- Herbert Kritzer, University of Minnesota Law School
- Geoffrey McGovern, RAND Corporation

3:00 p.m.   **Break**

3:15 p.m.   **Panel #4:** Access to Justice and B2B Litigation

Moderator: Geoffrey McGovern

- Rebecca Sandefur, University of Illinois College of Law
- Craig Holden, Lewis Brisbois Bisgaard & Smith
- Jeff Kichaven, Jeff Kichaven Commercial Mediation

4:15 p.m.   **Final Keynote Address**

William T. Robinson III, Frost Brown Todd; Co-Chair, ABA Task Force on Preservation of the Justice System

4:45 p.m.   **Closing Remarks**

Robert Peck

5:00 p.m.   **Reception in the RAND Library**

6:00 p.m.   **Event concludes**

2